DANGER Flying Objects!

KAROLYN KENDRICK

Steck
Vaughn™

A Harcourt Achieve Imprint

www.Steck-Vaughn.com
1-800-531-5015

Danger: Flying Objects!
By Karolyn Kendrick

Photo Acknowledgements
Cover ©Detlev Van Ravenswaay/Photo Researchers, Inc.; p. 3
©Denis Scott/CORBIS; p. 7 NASA/JPL/UMD Artwork by Pat
Rawlings; p. 8 ©Jon Lomberg/Photo Researchers, Inc.; p. 10–11
©D. Van Ravenswaay/Photo Researchers, Inc.; p. 15 ©Joe Skipper/
Reuters/CORBIS; p. 16 ©John R. Foster/Photo Researchers, Inc.;
p. 19 ©Julian Baum/Photo Researchers, Inc.; p.23 ©Denis Scott/
CORBIS; p. 28 ©NASA/Photo Researchers, Inc.

Illustration Acknowledgements
p. 4 Ted Nasmith; p. 13 Ken Batelman
p. 21 Barbara Massey; p. 25 Ted Nasmith

Steck-Vaughn is a trademark of Harcourt Achieve Inc.

Printed in China

2 3 4 5 6 7 8 1666 13 12 11

4500288216   BCDEF

ISBN-13: 978-1-4190-2302-6

Table of Contents

Introduction Space Rocks. 4

1 Deep Impact. 6

   The Whole World Is Watching 14

2 Collision Course 16

   Life from Outer Space? 22

3 Asteroid Hunters. 24

Glossary 30

Index. 32

Space Rocks

It was a June morning in 1908. High above Siberia in northern Asia, a rock from space came blasting toward Earth. The rock burst into flames above the ground. People from 60 kilometers (37.3 miles) away saw a fireball brighter than the sun.

The blast flattened 80 million trees. Animals fell over dead from the shock wave. The explosion was felt halfway around the world in Washington, DC. What was it?

Through **astronomy**, we have learned about the objects in our solar system. Along with the planets, billions of rocks speed through space around us. Like the planets, these rocks also **orbit** the sun.

Meteors are space rocks or space dust that enter Earth's **atmosphere**. Millions of these little pieces hit us each year. They look like shooting stars. Most of them burn up before they reach the ground. If a piece hits the earth, it's called a **meteorite**.

The explosion over Siberia was so strong that the space rock was blasted to bits. Scientists searched the site but never found a meteorite or a crater. It's still a bit of a mystery. Scientists do know one thing for sure. That wasn't the first time Earth was hit. And it won't be the last.

In 1908, a meteor exploded over Siberia in northern Asia. It had the power of a hydrogen bomb. The blast flattened about 8,000 square kilometers (3,089 square miles) of forest.

CHAPTER 1

Deep Impact

On July 4, 2005, astronomers around the world were **focused** on a tiny spacecraft called Deep Impact. It was the size of a car. Telescopes and other scientific devices stuck out from its sides. Deep Impact carried another craft beneath it. This craft was called the impactor. The impactor was the size of a washing machine.

Deep Impact had traveled 431 million kilometers (268 million miles) from Earth. Its mission was to find a space rock called a **comet**.

NASA had sent Deep Impact to take pictures and collect **data**. The scientists at NASA were seeking information about Comet Tempel 1. They wondered exactly what it was made of.

Why did they care? Scientists study comets because comets have probably been around as long as the solar system has existed. The study of comets may tell us more about how planets and stars formed. They may even tell us something about the development of life on Earth.

Deep Impact met up with the comet. When Tempel 1 lay directly ahead, the impactor was released.

The Deep Impact spacecraft collected and sent back important data from Comet Tempel 1. This illustration shows what the comet may have looked like just seconds after the impactor smashed into it.

Its rockets fired. The impactor moved even closer to the comet. It radioed pictures back to Earth.

KABOOM! The impactor hit its target. The blast had the force of 4.8 tons of dynamite. Gas and dust sprayed into space. It left a crater in the comet of nearly 200 meters (656 feet) in diameter. The impact lit up telescopes everywhere. To most scientists, it was better than any fireworks display.

For billions of years, comets have smashed into planets. But on this July 4th celebration, Earth reached out to hit a comet for the first time.

A Solar System Is Born

Here's how scientists explain the birth of our solar system. About 4.6 billion years ago, our solar system was just a spinning cloudy **nebula** of dust and gas. Then, scientists think a nearby star exploded. Shock waves pushed dust and gas together into a ball.

Over time, this ball began pulling more matter into it. That's the force of **gravity** at work. The gravitational force made the ball grow smaller and more tightly packed.

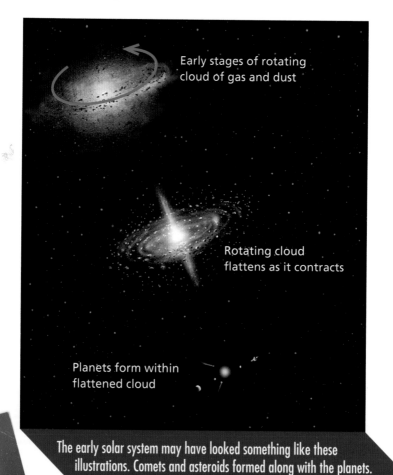

Early stages of rotating cloud of gas and dust

Rotating cloud flattens as it contracts

Planets form within flattened cloud

The early solar system may have looked something like these illustrations. Comets and asteroids formed along with the planets.

Pressure heated the center of the ball to 100° million C (180° million F). Our sun was being born.

Leftover dust and gas swirled around the baby sun. Dust, rock, ice, and metal particles crashed into each other and stuck. Some clumps grew bigger. As these clumps grew, they formed planets.

But some space rubble never became part of the sun or the planets. These chunks were mostly ice. Comets are these icy leftovers.

Billions of comets circle the sun. They travel so far from the sun's heat that they never thaw. They probably have not changed much in 4.6 billion years. This makes them ancient time capsules.

Force of Attraction

According to a popular tale, Newton watched an apple fall from a tree. He wondered, "Why didn't it just float in the air?" Newton thought that Earth must **exert** a force on the apple. That same force might also pull the moon toward Earth. In fact, it could even pull the planets toward the sun.

According to Newton, this force attracts all objects to each other. The force is known as gravity. The more **mass** an object has, the greater its gravitational force. Mass is the amount of **matter** in an object. The sun has enormous mass. It's able to hold planets in orbit, even from millions of miles away.

Asteroids are also created from space rubble. They are made of rock and metal. Most of them probably formed near the planet Jupiter. These space rocks travel at very high speeds. Today, billions of asteroids orbit the sun in the Asteroid Belt between Mars and Jupiter.

Sometimes asteroids and comets get knocked out of orbit. Asteroids crash into each other. The impact sends them shooting off into space. A comet may swing too close to one of the giant planets, like Jupiter or Saturn. The planet's gravity can pull the comet in a new direction.

Sometimes a comet gets knocked toward the sun. The comet heats up as it gets closer. Ice **evaporates** and turns to gas. The glowing gases and dust may stretch into a tail behind the comet. Every ten years or so, a comet comes close enough to Earth for us to see its tail without the aid of a powerful telescope.

Billions of years ago, space rocks probably came a lot closer than that. It is thought that they often hit our planet. Some scientists believe that comets may have brought water to our planet. They think that gift may have helped life develop. (See page 22.)

Uranus

Neptune

Earth

Pluto

Mercury

Venus

Mars

Saturn

Jupiter

Most comets circle the sun beyond the planet Pluto. Asteroids orbit the sun much closer to Earth. The Asteroid Belt lies between Mars and Jupiter. Billions are in orbit there.

Studying the Comet

The Deep Impact spacecraft is already helping us better understand comets. The impactor created a big crater. Gases and dust blasted into space. The gases glowed from the energy of the impact. Bright sunlight bounced off the huge dust cloud. In space and on Earth, telescopes caught the action.

The telescopes had **spectrometers** attached to them. These devices measure the temperature and **density** of distant objects. That's how scientists tell what the objects are made of.

Substances either reflect light or absorb it. Some substances even create their own light. A spectrometer measures the light from a substance.

Radio	Microwave	Infrared	Visible	Ultraviolet	X-ray	Gamma Ray
10^4 10^2	1		10^{-2}	10^{-5}	10^{-6}	10^{-8}	10^{-10} 10^{-12}

Wavelength in centimeters

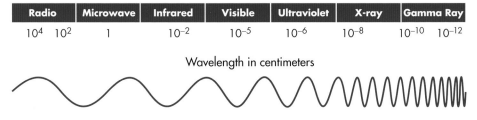

About the size of…

Buildings   Humans   Honey Bee   Pinhead   Protozoans   Molecules   Atoms   Atomic Nuclei

Every time you feel the sun's ultraviolet rays, hear a song on the radio, or make popcorn in the microwave, you're experiencing electromagnetic energy. This chart shows the types of electromagnetic energy.

Light energy travels in waves, like the waves in the ocean. Each kind of energy has a different **wavelength**. Wavelengths are measured from the top of one wave to the top of the next. Radio waves, for instance, have very long wavelengths. X-rays and gamma rays have very short wavelengths. The range of energy wavelengths from long to short is called a **spectrum**. Not all energy wavelengths can be seen with the human eye. The light energy we can see falls in the middle of the spectrum.

Each gas in Comet Tempel 1's dust cloud reflected light differently. The spectrometer showed a different pattern for each. Scientists are using these patterns to identify the substances in the comet.

It will take years to study all the images and data. Within three months, though, scientists had some results. They found that the comet was not solid. It was more like a flying pile of fine powder. They also discovered clay and carbon. These are the kinds of materials found in seashells here on Earth.

Scientists are already looking ahead. Europeans have launched the Rosetta spacecraft. It is scheduled to land on a comet in 2014. Scientists want to bring a sample of a comet back to Earth. In the meantime, Deep Impact has given them a lot to think about. "I can't believe they're paying us to have this much fun," said one researcher.

The Whole World Is Watching

Karen J. Meech studies comets at the University of Hawaii in Honolulu. She was a member of the Deep Impact research team.

I got hooked on space from watching *Star Trek* in second grade. Now, I study very far-off comets with the world's biggest telescopes. Comets are neat to look at because they are always changing.

For the Deep Impact mission, I was in charge of all telescope observations. But my job started long before the spacecraft was launched. Before we could hit Comet Tempel 1, we had to get to know it really well.

I started looking at Tempel 1 eight years before. We had to set a target area. We had to keep the Deep Impact spacecraft safe from dust. And we had to identify gases near the comet surface.

Getting time on big telescopes is really hard. But the idea of smashing a spacecraft into a comet was totally unique. We received 800 telescope nights to study Tempel 1. That's unheard of!

By impact day, the entire planet was watching. Space telescopes turned toward the comet. There were over 80 observatories in all. We linked mission control and observers by video. You could see and hear what was going on as the comet approached. We helped each other solve problems. Real-time data streamed in from space to telescopes around the world. People wanted to be a part of this because they could actually see it happen.

The moment of impact was thrilling. We hit a bull's-eye!

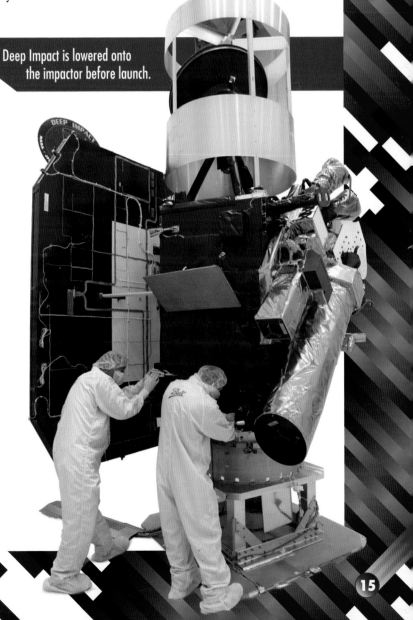

Deep Impact is lowered onto the impactor before launch.

A space rock like this one may have caused the extinctiion of the dinosaurs.

 Collision Course

Dinosaurs ruled Earth for 160 million years. Then, they vanished. For 65 million years after that, their bones were buried in the ground. Layer after layer of dirt collected on top of them. Over time, pressure turned the bones into stone fossils.

In the 1800s, scientists began to dig up the fossilized dinosaur bones. They also examined the layers of dirt. They noticed two special layers. The lower layer of dirt is where dinosaur fossils are found. With those fossils are the remains of other **extinct** plants and animals.

The layer of dirt above that one shows evidence of a great change. It happened about 65 million years ago. In this layer, there are no dinosaur fossils. Instead, fossils of new plants and animals appear. Some of these species still exist today.

Scientists call the line between the two layers the K-T boundary. It holds the clue to one of the biggest disasters that ever happened on Earth. About the time this layer formed, something killed off 60 percent of all the plant and animal species on Earth.

For a long time, this was one of science's biggest mysteries. Today, some scientists have a theory. Maybe a space rock caused this great change.

Solving the Riddle

A father-son team may have solved the mystery. Earth scientist Walter Alvarez was digging in Italy in the 1970s. He found a thin layer of clay along the K-T boundary. Walter's father, Luis, worked with scientists to examine the clay layer. It contained a metal called iridium. Iridium is rare on Earth's surface. It exists in larger amounts deep underground. It's also found in space dust.

How did iridium get into the K-T boundary? Why don't we find it anywhere else ?

Walter and Luis considered the possibilities. Maybe a star exploded far out in space. The blast could have sent iridium raining down on Earth. Maybe huge volcanic eruptions spit out the metal.

The Alvarez team had another **hypothesis**. They thought the evidence pointed to a space rock. Either an asteroid or a comet might have hit Earth. This wouldn't have been a tiny meteorite. It would have been at least 10 kilometers (6 miles) in diameter. The impact would have caused massive destruction. It would also have left behind plenty of iridium.

A piece of the puzzle was still missing. The impact would have created a huge crater. The scientists searched the maps to find one large enough. They couldn't find one that fit.

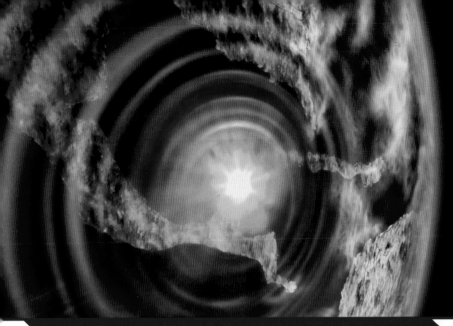

This is what the Chicxulub impact might have looked like from space.

In 1990, researchers found a huge crater. It lay hidden just off the coast of Mexico under the Caribbean Sea. It was about the right age. The giant hole stretches nearly 280 kilometers (174 miles) from rim to rim. Its **depth** reaches 900 meters (3,000 feet). The scientists named it Chicxulub (CHEECH-uh-loob) after a nearby village. The Alvarezes had their evidence.

The Chicxulub impact probably released 10 billion times the energy of the first nuclear bomb. Imagine it! The sky burns. Rocks melt. The blast smashes coral reefs. It flattens forests. It spreads carbon dioxide and other gases throughout the atmosphere. Giant **tsunami** waves race out from the crash.

The impact would have been deadly. Still, could it have killed off 60 percent of the species on Earth?

Extinction Time

The Alvarezes described how the impact may have caused so much damage. Dust and gases from the explosion circled the globe. They shut out sunlight for months. Without sunlight, plants could not grow. Plant-eaters had nothing to eat. The world's **food chain** would be broken.

The food chain is **vital** to life on Earth. It begins with the sun. Plants need sunlight to make food. They soak up water through their roots. They take in carbon dioxide through their leaves. The sun's energy is used to turn water and carbon dioxide into sugar.

Plants use the food energy from the sugar to grow. **Mammals** and other animals get some of this food energy by eating plants. The plant-eaters then get eaten by meat-eating animals. The energy is passed on from link to link in the food chain. Each link depends on another link for its survival. Break a link, and **resources** become scarce. Species that cannot change and adapt will die.

Some scientists disagree with the Alvarezes. They claim the dinosaurs were dying before the impact. They say volcanoes could have caused Earth's climate to change. Still, most people agree that space rocks probably played a role.

Collisions have had a huge effect on Earth. Craters have been found all across the globe. Some scientists think impacts cause mass extinctions about every five million years.

The worst extinction happened 245 million years ago. Sea levels dropped. Water temperatures rose. About 95 percent of sea life died. About 70 percent of large land species disappeared.

These theories have some people asking, "When will the next big space rock hit?"

Many craters were caused by meteorites hitting the earth.

Life from Outer Space?

Comets and asteroids have done plenty of damage to life on Earth. Yet, scientists think they may have helped create life in the first place.

When Earth first formed, it was hot, bare, and rocky. No life existed. Volcanoes spewed out heat and gases. Asteroids crashed down. Temperatures ran so high that most water boiled away. It evaporated and remained a gas.

About four billion years ago, the planet began to cool down. Oceans filled with water. Soon after, life appeared on Earth.

Much of that early water came from volcanoes. It blasted out as water vapor. When Earth cooled, the vapor **condensed** back into water as rain.

Some astronomers think that Earth's water supply may have gotten help from outer space. Comets are mostly frozen water. When they smashed into Earth, they added to the water already here.

Scientists are working to test this theory. Karen Meech from the Deep Impact project is searching for ancient comet water. She and others are drilling in Hawaii and Iceland. They hope to find water in deep, ancient rocks. They'll test the water for chemicals. They'll see if these chemicals match those found on Comet Tempel 1 and other comets.

Water may not be the only gift from the comets. Life on Earth needs carbon, too. Carbon is an element found in every living thing.

Comets are rich in carbon. Many scientists think Earth may not have had enough carbon to get life started. Carbon compounds from space could have been the building blocks of life.

How life started is still a great mystery. Earth has all the right pieces of the puzzle. It is the right distance from the sun. It has just the right atmosphere and temperature. Water exists as a liquid here. (It boils away on Venus and freezes on Mars.) Earth may have needed just one more ingredient: carbon. Maybe a comet supplied it.

Space rocks sometimes pass very near our planet.

CHAPTER 3

Asteroid Hunters

On January 13, 2004, the world was almost put on high alert. A telescope in New Mexico spotted an asteroid. It looked to be heading right toward Earth.

The rock probably wasn't big enough to cause a mass extinction. Yet, it could have exploded in the atmosphere. The force might equal the 1908 blast in northern Asia. If it blew up near a city, it could have killed thousands of people.

Scientists weren't sure of the asteroid's course. They needed more data. One researcher predicted that it could hit Earth in as little as 36 hours. Experts weren't sure how close the asteroid would come. It was a tense time for astromoners and other space researchers.

The asteroid didn't hit Earth after all. It passed about 13 million kilometers (8 million miles) away. That's 33 times the distance between Earth and the moon. We were lucky.

We were never in danger. Still, that didn't make everyone feel safe. All around the globe, space watchers have fixed their eyes on the sky since then. They search for asteroids that might hit us. We may not need an early warning in our lifetimes. If we do, though, it could save millions of lives.

Search Teams

The United States has five groups searching for space rocks. Each one scans the sky in a different way. Robert McMillan is an astronomer with a group called SpaceWatch. "SpaceWatch looks for the very faint objects," he says. "That means they're either very far away or very small. We need a long warning time if a big asteroid is on the way."

Asteroid hunters use powerful telescopes. Every 30 minutes they take pictures of the sky. Then, they compare the images. Stars never move. They appear in the same place from image image. Against this background, the asteroids are easy to spot. They change position relative to the stars.

Find the asteroid. Astronomers map asteroids by comparing images of the sky. Where is the asteroid in these images?

Asteroid hunters spend long nights at their telescopes. They have identified about 65 percent of the space rocks in our solar system. These asteroids measure at least 1 kilometer (0.6 miles) in diameter. About 1,000 of them orbit near Earth. Asteroids this size could wipe out entire countries. A 20-kilometer (12-mile) asteroid could cause a mass extinction.

A comet hit Jupiter in 1994. Jupiter's gravitational pull is many times stronger than Earth's. It sucked in Comet Shoemaker-Levy. The comet

The Danger from Asteroids This graph shows the relationship between the frequency and size of impacts. It's called the Shoemaker Curve.

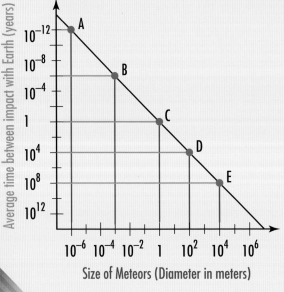

Shoemaker Curve

Average time between impact with Earth (years)

Size of Meteors (Diameter in meters)

A. Dust-sized particles hit the surface of the space shuttle every 30 milliseconds.

B. Shooting stars occur every 30 seconds.

C. Meteorites about one meter (1.09 yards) in diameter hit Earth each year.

D. Asteroids about 100 meters (109 yards) in diameter hit Earth every 10,000 years or so. These are big enough to destroy a city.

E. Every 100,000,000 years or so, an asteroid about 10 kilometers (6 miles) in diameter will hit Earth. An asteroid this size caused the Chicxulub crater.

broke apart and smashed into the planet. Giant fireballs flared up. One piece of the comet crashed with terrible force. It carried 750 times the energy of all the nuclear weapons on Earth.

Asteroid hunters have a harder time finding smaller space rocks. They **estimate** there are about 25,000 rocks that measure 100–220 meters (109–219 yards) in diameter. These rocks could destroy a city.

What are the chances of another big collision soon? Not very high. Huge asteroids hit maybe once every 10 million years. The smaller ones arrive about every 10,000 years. According to McMillan, "There's no known asteroid in sight that is really dangerous."

By 2007, telescopes will be scanning the entire night sky. This will improve our early-warning system. "You can warn people about hurricanes, tsunamis, tornadoes, and even earthquakes," says McMillan. "But you can't do anything about them. Except get out of the way."

Could we do more to protect ourselves from asteroids? Space scientists are developing plans now. Perhaps a rocket could land on an approaching asteroid. Robots would plant rockets on the surface. Then, the rockets would **propel** the asteroid into a new orbit. Earth would be safe. But McMillan thinks we would need fifty years' warning. That's why he's watching the far-off asteroids.

Space Resources

In the future, we may think of asteroids as resources, not threats. Many asteroids contain valuable metals. They hold frozen helium and methane for rocket fuel. They have ice for drinking water.

Humans may soon pay a visit to an asteroid. "It's easier to visit an asteroid than to land on the moon," says McMillan. Unlike the moon, asteroids don't have much gravity to overcome. A spacecraft could land and take off easily. An unmanned probe landed on an asteroid in 2001.

Still, there will be challenges. Space contains no air. It's a **vacuum**. Astronauts must carry oxygen with them in tanks. They can't carry enough. A voyage to the Asteroid Belt would take four years.

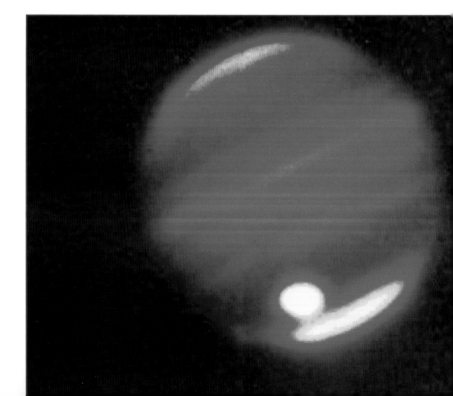

Astronauts could make oxygen on the way. Submarine crews create oxygen from water. Water is two parts hydrogen and one part oxygen. Electricity is used to create a chemical reaction. It separates the hydrogen from the oxygen. The oxygen can then be used for breathing.

The other problem comes from a lack of gravity. In space, astronauts are almost weightless. They float. They have to work, eat, and drink in "zero-gravity." Long duration space flights can cause muscle loss. On Earth, astronauts train in a giant swimming pool. It's the size of a football field. Underwater, the astronauts use SCUBA gear to breathe.

Human beings also need air pressure. In space, there is none. Without air pressure, gases in the body expand. They spread out to fill the vacuum. To protect the body, spaceships and spacesuits must be pressurized, or filled with air.

All these problems can be solved. Yet, we may not even need astronauts to make use of asteroids. Someday robots could do the asteroid mining for us.

Researchers like Robert McMillan and Karen Meech want to unlock the secrets of space rocks. They hope to find the story of our distant past. They also want to protect us from collisions. They hope to turn asteroids and comets from deadly threats into useful resources.

Comet Shoemaker-Levy collided with Jupiter in 1994. This was the first collision of a comet and planet ever to be observed.

Glossary

asteroid *(noun)* a piece of rock that travels in an orbit around the sun

astronomy *(noun)* the science of stars, planets, and space

atmosphere *(noun)* the layers of gases surrounding a planet

collision *(noun)* the crashing together of two objects

comet *(noun)* a celestial object that travels through space with a long tail

condense *(verb)* to turn a gas into a liquid

data *(noun)* information or facts

density *(noun)* an object's mass divided by its volume; a measure of how tightly packed particles in an object are

depth *(noun)* how deep something is

estimate *(verb)* to make an approximate calculation of something

evaporate *(verb)* to change from a liquid to a gas

exert *(verb)* bring to bear; act on something

extinct *(adjective)* no longer living, as in an entire species

focus *(verb)* to concentrate on something

food chain *(noun)* the order in which animals and plants feed on other animals and plants

gravity *(noun)* a force that attracts all objects to all other objects

hypothesis *(noun)* a theory or prediction that can be tested

mammal *(noun)* a warm-blooded animal that has a backbone

mass *(noun)* the amount of matter that something contains

matter *(noun)* anything that has mass and takes up space, including solids, liquids, and gases

meteor *(noun)* a piece of rock or metal from space that enters Earth's atmosphere

meteorite *(noun)* a part of a meteor that falls to Earth before burning up

nebula *(noun)* a bright cloud in space made of gases, dust, or stars

orbit *(verb)* to circle around a planet or star or other object in space

pressure *(noun)* the force produced by pressing on something

propel *(verb)* to move forward or onward

resource *(noun)* something that can be used to satisfy a need

spectrometer *(noun)* a device that measures the wavelengths of light energy

spectrum *(noun)* the range of things, as light energy with different wavelengths

tsunami *(noun)* a huge wave caused by an undersea earthquake or volcano

vital *(adjective)* extremely important

wavelength *(noun)* the distance between two crests in a series of waves

vacuum *(noun)* a place in which there is no air

Idioms

hooked on *(page 14)* to be very interested in something
I am hooked on comic books.

Index

Alvarez, Luis, 18–20
Alvarez, Walter, 18–20
asteroids, 4, 10, 18, 22, 24–29
astronomers, 6
atmosphere, 4, 19, 23

carbon, 13, 23
collisions, 21
comets, 4, 6–7, 9–10, 12–15, 18, 22–23, 26, 29

data, 6, 13, 15
Deep Impact, 6–7, 12–15, 22
density, 12
dinosaurs, 17, 20

evaporate, 10, 22
extinction, 17, 20–21, 24

food chain, 20

gravity, 8, 9, 10, 29

hypothesis, 18

K–T boundary, 17–21

mammals, 20
mass, 9
McMillan, Robert, 25, 27, 28, 29
Meech, Karen J., 14–15, 22, 29
meteorites, 4–5, 18, 21
meteors, 4

nebula, 8
Newton, Isaac, 9

orbit, 4

pressure, 8, 29

resources, 20, 28, 29

solar system, 4, 6, 8–10
spectrometers, 12–13
spectrum, 13

tsunami, 19

vacuum, 28, 29

wavelength, 13